cover to cover

Unexpected
Jesus

CWR

Anna Robbins

Contents

INTRODUCTION

Have you ever received a large package in the post and opened it with excitement, only to discover that there was yet another box and simply too much packaging for the small and unimpressive item it contained? The big surprise failed to meet your expectations.

'Not as expected' often means that the reality turns out to be less exciting than we'd hoped. Maybe you ordered a cake or bought an item only to be disappointed by its diminutive size and diminished appearance.

However, a 'not as expected' experience can sometimes be positive. Maybe you've gone to an event, thinking you'd rather be at home in bed with a book. It's a cold wet evening but you pushed yourself to go, and it ended up being one of the best nights of your life! You expected something dull and uninteresting, and you got something that surpassed all expectations.

A well-known Advent hymn issues the invitation, 'Come, thou long-expected Jesus'. But when Jesus showed up, He overturned and surpassed all hopes of what He would be and do. Although the arrival of a messiah was prophesied by some, Jesus was certainly *not* what most people were expecting. For the Pharisees, He was the total opposite of the kind of saviour they had imagined, and they quickly set about trying to discredit and get rid of Him. For the poor, blind and bound, His arrival was the best news possible. Those who met Him never left unchallenged or unchanged. For many, the encounter carried the potential of total – and unexpected – transformation.

Today, bombarded by the reality of an unexpected global pandemic, our unsustainable impact on the planet, our abuse of people and crumbling political institutions, perhaps we find it difficult to muster any sort of positive expectation whatsoever. Generally, as a people, we have surrendered to the paraphrased words of the eighteenth-century poet Alexander Pope: 'Blessed are those who expect nothing, for they will never be disappointed.' In the context of our lives, do we dare to invite the presence of an unexpected Jesus?

Over these days together, we will consider the prophets' expectations of Jesus; how Jesus' arrival on the scene was completely unexpected, and how those around Him were transformed as a result. We will explore some encounters Jesus had with people who were faced with His unexpected presence and the searching power of His love. As we see how they responded, hopefully we too will be challenged to respond.

What are *your* expectations this Advent? Are you keeping them low in order to avoid disappointment? This Christmas, instead of thinking about what you expect from others, think about what you expect from God. What does it mean that God is with you, right now?

Come and meet an unexpected Jesus – and never be the same again.

How to use this book:

This book is designed to be read each day alongside your Bible. Choose a time of day that is best for you, where you can have a few quiet moments to yourself. There are 31 days of readings, so you can read it daily through the month of December, or you can pick it up at any time and go at your own pace. Begin your time with a brief prayer, inviting the Lord to meet with you through His Word.

For each day, there is a Bible reading and a reflection related to the passage. There are suggestions for further Bible passages to ponder, questions to consider that will hopefully help you apply the readings to your own life and a closing prayer.

If you are using this book as part of a small group, it's helpful if each member has their own copy to read throughout the week. Group leaders may find the group study notes at the back of the book to be a helpful resource for preparing and leading each session.

SESSION ONE

Great Expectations

DAY 1

Unexpectedly with us

Bible Reading

Genesis 1:26–31

Daily Focus

There is a series of stained-glass windows in the chapel of the university where I work depicting the gospel story from Genesis through to the birth, life and death of Jesus. The first window, however, doesn't begin the story with creation but a sorrowful picture of Adam and Eve leaving the garden, humiliated, and with the serpent slithering in the background. According to designer of the windows, that is where the gospel starts – with the Fall.

Often, for us, the gospel starts to impact us at our lowest point too. We are so aware of our fallenness, our unworthiness, our shame and our failures that we wonder, even if there is God, why should He be mindful of us, of me? At the beginning of this Advent season, the words that spoke creation into being deserve to be lingered over because they hold the power of life.

The book of Genesis reveals that we have a relationship with God and the capacity to relate to Him because He created us in His own image. This mystery is a fundamental quality that we all share as human beings, across ethnicities and other identities. 'God saw all that he had made, and it was very good' (v31). Declaring the creation 'good' doesn't mean it was perfect. Rather, it means it was fitting for the purpose for which it was made. Creation functioned as it should. It did what He purposed it to do.

All of creation was designed to function well. The tree of life is positioned at the centre of the Garden (Gen. 2:9). Death is kept at a distance. Goodness is our default. Maybe that's why we often seem to have an inbuilt sense that things are not always the way they *should* be. We long for the goodness of the Garden, where the creator walked with His people

(Gen. 3:8). This is the beginning of the story: God with us. He's always been with us. His desire is to always be with us.

God at work in creation is the first pane in the window of our gospel story. 'God with us' is the first theological affirmation of humanity in creation. In a culture of negativity, which often feels so dark, we have an unexpected reminder that the light is not far away. 'The LORD is my light and my salvation – whom shall I fear' (Psa. 27:1).

Ponder
Psalm 27

Questions to Consider
If you had a window with different panes telling the story of the gospel at work in your life, what would the first pane look like? How does that picture reveal your expectations of how God relates to you? Do you expect that God desires to walk with you in the reality of your everyday life?

Closing Prayer
Thank You, Father, that You've wanted to be with us from the beginning. Help me to accept that You want to be with me even in the mess of real life, and that nothing in my life surprises You. Remind me this season, when so much seems not to be the way it should be, that You created the world for good. Amen.

DAY 2

Unexpected consequences

Bible Reading

Genesis 3

Daily Focus

Things had been going so well. Creation was functioning as God had purposed it to work. Adam and Eve were relating rightly to one another, to creation and to the creator. As image-bearers, they were accountable to God for what He gave them to look after; they ate from a tree of life that enabled them to live forever; they had everything they could ever need – but they wanted more. Unfulfilled desire clouded their judgment, and they no longer trusted God for their lives.

The serpent introduced the idea that maybe, just maybe, they could expand their horizons and push back their limitations. They could be like God, having more knowledge and more power. A ravenous craving awakened in them. And their relationships that had been good became unexpectedly bad. They thought they would achieve something great on their own, away from the one who had designed them for connection with Him and each other. Instead, their connections dropped and relationships crumbled.

Not only did they now feel shame in their friendship with God but their bond with each other was also broken. The way that men and women relate became dysfunctional. Their song of harmony with the rest of creation was disrupted. Enmity, rather than unity, ruled the day. Instead of creation functioning together with an organic hum, it began to groan.

Now as then, creation groans not in complaint of what is past, but in expectation of a renewal that is to come. It groans in labour pains of new birth (Rom. 8:22). And with the expectation of a future birthed and nurtured by God, there is hope. Our sense that the world isn't as it *should* be is a sign that God is not finished with us yet. C.S. Lewis attributes this sense as a key to his conversion to the Christian faith – that there had to be a standard against which to measure the lack of justice in the world. Rather than evidence against God's presence, our awareness of the world being imperfect suggests He is still calling us to Himself.

The poet Francis Thompson described God as the 'hound of heaven'. We see in the Garden of Eden that we are the ones who hide from God, while He seeks after us with His love and grace. The narrative of the Old Testament unfolds in an ongoing story of hide and seek, where people repeatedly hide from God, while He constantly chases after them with His arms open.

Despite human rebellion, and our rugged pursuit of self-reliance, God is undeniably present. And it's not only God who longs for a renewed relationship with His people: creation groans in eager expectation of healing and wholeness to come, awaiting a new birth.

Ponder
Psalm 139:1–12

Questions to Consider
In what ways do you rebel against God's call on your life? How do you experience the brokenness of relationships between creation, people and God? Can you think of a time when you thought God was hiding, only to discover that He was searching after you?

Prayer
Thank You, God, that Your grace and mercy are wider than I could ever fathom. Forgive me when I think my plans for my life are better than Yours. Renew my expectations so that I can see You at work in the world, and in my life. Birth in me a new hope. Amen.

DAY 3

God on my terms?

Bible Reading

Genesis 11:1–9

Daily Focus

By the time we reach Genesis 11, the wilful individual rebellion of Adam and Eve in Genesis 3 becomes a full-blown attempt by the community in Shinar (v2) to take charge of God. The structures of creation and the inter-relations of human and divine life are clearly broken.

In today's reading, we find God's people no longer satisfied with living on His terms, within the boundaries He set for them. They see the cultures around them building large towers where their gods will come to live and do their bidding. They wonder why they should not become the most powerful people with the most powerful God.

So they build a tower.

They expect God to come and live in their tower and do all the things they ask of Him. This would indeed make them the strongest, most famous people in all the land: 'we may make a name for ourselves', they say (v4). They don't want a God where they must surrender to His terms, His plans for their lives. They want a god who will give them power and wealth – immediate satisfaction.

God comes down and has a look at what they've built. He is not pleased. But He doesn't crush them. Instead He scatters them and confuses their language in order to diminish their pride and prevent further rebellion. He doesn't want to destroy them. He just wants them to come to Him on His terms rather than their own; to remember that He is God and they are not. Despite the heights of their arrogance, He does not leave them.

His faithfulness is unexpectedly eternal, even in the face of our constant shortcomings. We too want God to do what we want Him to do. We want to pull the strings and push the buttons. When He doesn't do what we expect, we put God on trial. *Why have You not saved those people? How can You let those ones suffer?* These are genuine questions but we treat the creator of the universe as though He belongs in a box (or a tower) where He is answerable to us and responsible to do our bidding.

If we are to calibrate our expectations of God biblically, we will be reminded that *we* are answerable to the God of the universe, and not the other way around. Even in the face of rebellion, God is still with His people. Even when the entire community at Babel attempted to take control of God for their own ends, He did not abandon them. Neither has He abandoned us.

The world is messy and fallen, and this reality conditions our expectations, as it should. Every day we experience the fractured relationships of a fallen creation impacted by sin. However, even in the midst of our rebellion against God and our attempts to control Him for our own purposes, He has never let us go. Unexpectedly, God is *still* with us.

Ponder
Joshua 1:5–7

Questions to Consider
In what ways do you want God to be God on your terms? In what ways are you prone to make God in your image rather than be conformed to His? As you look back on your own life, can you identify times when God refused to let you go?

Closing Prayer
Forgive me, Lord, when I seek to make You my servant, rather than to serve You. Help me to remember that even when I have rebelled against You, You have never abandoned me. Teach me to trust that You will never let me go. Amen.

DAY 4

What does God want from me?

Bible Reading
Hosea 1:1–11

Daily Focus
Human relationships can be confusing as we try to figure out what another person wants from us. Our relationship with God can sometimes be the same. We do what we think is right, but we're not sure we can trust His faithfulness, His love. We're not sure what He wants.

The Old Testament book of Hosea tells an unusual story about God and His relationship with His people. It's a gripping account of unfaithfulness and loyalty; of rebellion and love; of wandering and wooing.

God tells the prophet Hosea to take a prostitute for a wife and have children with her. The children's names represent God's pity, punishment and relational pain. They refer to the way that God's people have persistently done their own thing, and how God has constantly chased after them and defended them. In the face of their unfaithfulness, His love is endless. But it doesn't come without personal cost. The third child's name sums up the emotion of the fraught relationship: 'you are not my people, and I am not your God' (v9).

Perhaps there have been times in your life when you felt (and maybe still feel) that God expected too much and demanded too much. Maybe you felt the cost of following Him was too much and either ignored or went against God, and now you wonder if He can forgive you. Imagine the pain of hearing from Him, 'You are not my child, and I am not your God.' *Is it true? Has He broken off the relationship forever?*

Like the people of Israel, represented by Hosea's unfaithful wife Gomer, we too reject God's call on our lives and turn to do our own thing.

The people of Israel were worshipping false gods, neglecting justice, denying what God had done for them. He wasn't simply embarrassed by His children, like a mum with a screaming child, having a tantrum in a café. He was pointing out that they had denied their very DNA. They were created in His image, for relationship with Him, as individuals and a community. No matter how many times He went after them and brought them back, still they wandered off.

'You are not my people, and I am not your God' is painful to read, to think, to feel. It can't get much worse than being rejected by your creator. However, the final verses of the chapter reveal that this is not the end of the story but the beginning. The prophet tells us that the declaration: 'you are not my people' will be transformed into 'children of the living God' (v10). The break in relationship is the result of Israel's disobedience. They will be exiled from the Promised Land but they will be brought back, they will be healed. God will call them His children again.

We too may have turned away from God. Perhaps you have gone your own way many times. But God hasn't let you go. *What do You want from me anyway?* you might shout at Him like a petulant child, a broken-hearted lover, a confused soul.

Unexpectedly, just when things seem at their worst, God speaks and says, *My child.*

Ponder
Luke 15:11–32

Questions to Consider
In what ways do you struggle to stay faithful in your relationship with God? What does it mean to you that God calls you His child no matter how often you've rebelled?

Closing Prayer
Lord, I don't always know what You want from me, but I believe You do not let me go. Thank You for Your persistent and faithful love. Help me to grasp what it means to be Your loved child. Amen.

DAY 5

The wilderness

Bible Reading

Hosea 2:14–23

Daily Focus

The second chapter of Hosea continues, in poetic form, the themes addressed in the first chapter. Here God is portrayed as the faithful husband who pursues His promiscuous wife, to care for her, and ultimately to bring her back home. When the wife leaves her faithful husband, she goes off to pursue her lovers, looking for all the things they can provide for her – food, drink, luxuries. The husband is rightly upset. She had all of those luxuries, but never realised that he 'was the one who gave her the grain, the new wine and oil, who lavished on her the silver and gold' (v8). So he will hedge her in, and tenderly beckon her into the wilderness (v14).

We often think of the wilderness as a place of punishment, of spiritual dryness and testing. We describe spiritual wildernesses as places where God seems absent, or at least distant, and where we are harshly tested and very much alone. But the vision of the wilderness in Hosea is not like that. The wilderness is the place where the husband woos his wife, so that the distractions of life are removed. Here he can speak tenderly to her of vineyards, renewal and hope. The wilderness is where God can show how He keeps 'her' safe, how He brings love, justice and peace. What an unexpected picture of the wilderness! This would challenge the ways that the Israelites had experienced exile. God unexpectedly reframes their experience – from His perspective.

If you find yourself in a spiritual wilderness this Advent season, consider for a moment how God might show up in the midst of it. Perhaps He hasn't cast you out into the wilderness at all. Maybe the wilderness is a place where distractions are stripped away and He can speak tenderly to you. Perhaps He is there with you even now, whispering of refreshment, fruitfulness, love, justice and peace. Maybe this is also a picture for the Church in western culture at the moment. Living in an increasingly complex world often leaves us feeling as though we are in a wilderness together as Christians. Are we cast out of God's favour? Or has He wooed us to a place where our layers of false spirituality, prideful trust in human power and consumer distractions are stripped away? Could this wilderness be a good place for us, a refining place where, released from misplaced hopes, our faithfulness to Christ is renewed?

Listen for the voice of God. He is whispering to us of His faithfulness. He is beckoning us to return to Him. He is taking from our mouths and our worship the voices of false gods: empire, money, injustice and conflict. He asks us to know Him again. Do you hear His unexpected declaration spoken over us? 'You are my people.' May we have the courage, in the Spirit of Christ, to renew our vows: 'You are my God.'

Ponder
John 21:15–19

Questions to Consider
When have you experienced a spiritual wilderness? Where was God in that experience?

Closing Prayer
Lord, I thank You that You are the one who has always provided for me, and who has always loved me. Forgive me for when I have leaned on my own strength and failed to see what You have done. Make me willing today to give up some of the things I cling to that keep me from depending more on You. Help me to say, 'You are my God' with my whole life. Amen.

DAY 6

Groan to the Lord

Bible Reading

Joel 1:13–20

Daily Focus

When Adam and Eve set a course of disobedience for humanity, it didn't just impact their relationships with God and one another. It also interrupted the harmony of creation. When things go wrong between God and His people, there are consequences that are wreaked on the land, the water, plants, animals and sky. Creation groans.

As God's people continually wandered away from Him, even though He constantly chased after them, they repeated patterns of behaviour that defied the love of God for all that He had made. They disowned the gift of stewardship to care for creation, as part of creation. As we saw in previous readings, God's children had neglected justice and mercy. The poor were oppressed, and the land was not given its sabbath rest. Human rebellion had consequences for the whole earth.

So, here in Joel, we encounter a call to lament not only the exile of God's people, but the ruin of the country that has resulted from a failure to live well with God, each other and the land. Maybe we did not expect to see a prophetic call in the Bible to lament that the Promised Land is now a wasteland. While some of the animal imagery is no doubt reflecting the military conquest that took place, it is clear that the prophet connects faithfulness with blessing on the earth. This is not some sort of magic formula. Rather, it indicates that living well with God and others also means treating the land with justice and righteousness. It will flourish, as they flourish.

In many ways, we have failed to see that how we treat the earth is a reflection of our relationship with God. We have sought to provide for ourselves, rather than trust His provision. We have treated people and the planet with careless exploitation to meet the needs of the strong. Where are the qualities of justice and mercy that He requires?

Today, many cry out with the earth as it groans with the burden we have placed upon it. We have not allowed the land to rest, nor the ocean habitats to thrive. Sadly, it is the poorest who bear the greatest burden and worst consequences. It is all a clear indication that we have not been walking well with God. We have neglected our call. It is easier to hide and sleep than to tend to the overwhelming urgency of caring for our planet.

Nevertheless, Joel offers us an unexpected wake-up call that echoes down through the ages. Today the call to care for our planet comes most often from well-known environmentalists rather than the Church, and we are sometimes surprised when we discover it in Scripture. However, at times of greatest darkness and deepest destruction, God is present. Rather than abandoning His people, He invites repentance. Wake up! Lament! Cry out to God! It's not simply a cry of desperation. It is an act of worship; an expression of expectation.

Ponder
Romans 8:18–30

Questions to Consider
How do you pray when you feel overwhelmed by the needs of the world? What are some ways that you can turn your prayers of lament into prayers of action?

Closing Prayer
Father, forgive us. Wake us up to the consequences of neglect. When we do not have the words to pray, intercede by Your Spirit with groanings that go deeper still. Amen.

DAY 7

Where is your God?

Bible Reading

Joel 2:12–17

Daily Focus

'Where is God?' is the question often asked when things look grim and the world seems dark. In Joel's context, things *had* become bad. Really bad. God's people had been exiled from Israel. The land had been laid to waste by conquering forces, abuse and environmental destruction. It seemed like the end of the world. 'God, where are You?' was likely the cry that went up more than any other. Except for the mocking cry of their captors. *Hah! It was all well and good when things were well for you. But look around. You're in captivity, your milk and honey are dried up, and the locusts are eating the leftovers. Where is your God now?!*

Despite evidence to the contrary, Joel turns the issue back to an internal problem rather than external reality. If the outside world needed to be renewed, it would happen by means of an internal transformation first. 'Don't tear your clothing... tear your hearts instead' (v13, NLT) is the instruction. Tearing clothing was something those who were fasting might do as a demonstration of repentance. It could easily become a showy display of how spiritual someone was. The prophet tells the people this is a matter of flesh, not of fashion.

Turn back to the Lord, make a change of heart. The prophet recalls what he knows of God. *Yes, things look pretty bleak, and all hope seems lost. But remember,* he tells the people, *the Lord is gracious and merciful, slow to anger and abounding in steadfast love; He relents from punishing. Maybe He will again this time. Maybe.*

In Scripture, the notion of turning back to God is always upheld as an open possibility. The words of the prophet Joel, and other biblical prophets, are not easy. The judgment of God on the disobedience of His people is real. The consequences of their actions must be borne. The call to repent is as difficult as it is unexpected. But the invitation is made. In the midst of devastation, the prophets encourage the people to give it one last try and not let the last word be given to the sceptics and mockers. 'Why should they say among the people, "Where is their God?"' (v17).

When is the last time you asked, 'Where are You, God?' Maybe you gave up on asking Him anymore. Or maybe you're not confident that He can do anything significant about the state of the world or the chaos of your life anyway. Remember that He is a God of compassion and mercy. It's clear that Joel isn't certain that God will save them. But he is certain that God is exactly who He has shown Himself to be in the past. Joel is hoping for an intervention, an act of salvation. He will get something so much more than he expected. But it will take some time. The prophets fell silent for a long time. Sometimes God still seems silent for a long time.

When Jesus was crucified, He cried out, 'My God, my God, why have you forsaken me? (Mark 15:34). Let's take comfort from the fact that Jesus Himself knew what it felt like when God seems silent. But this Advent let's also remember that through the Holy Spirit God is *always* with us.

Ponder
Mark 15:16–34

Questions to Consider
What do you say to people when they ask, 'Where is your God?' When did you last ask, 'Where is my God?' How do you lean into your faith when God seems silent?

Closing Prayer
Sometimes I don't know where You are God. When You are silent, help me to recall Your faithfulness in the past and to draw courage from Your consistent character. Remind me You are here, even when You seem far away. Amen.

DAY 8

It's not you, it's me

Bible Reading
Micah 6:1–16

Daily Focus
After hearing Joel's prophecies, the people of Israel might have seemed distressed about the state of things between them and God but there was no significant change in their behaviour. God's people were indeed calling out to Him for mercy. But they were also cheating the poor in order to profit financially, and then going to worship as though God had no idea what they were up to. Micah boldly points out their hypocrisy: *Crying out to God in worship to fix the state of the world while living as you wish is not acceptable.*

Anyone who has ever been ripped off, short-changed or badly treated, knows how powerless it can feel if there is no recourse for appeal. God had showed His character of justice consistently throughout Israel's history. The people of Israel had been the recipients of ill-treatment and they knew that God was the defender of the powerless. Still, when it suited them, they were content to treat others unjustly and without mercy.

As the Old Testament ends, God reminds everyone of who He is, and what He expects of His people. It is not complicated, or difficult to comprehend but throughout their history, His people have seemed to find it very difficult to follow. 'He has shown you, O mortal, what is good. And what does the LORD require of you? To act justly, and to love mercy and to walk humbly with your God' (v8).

It's laid out clearly. This is what He expects. He has not failed. He is not hidden. *Why have His people avoided it? Why have they so often done the opposite? Why in the face of His faithfulness have they insisted on rebellion and destruction? Why hasn't He given up on them? Why hasn't He given up on me?*

While we've been asking God where He is, He has been asking us where we are. We think He is absent, but we are the ones who have wandered away while He stands waiting in expectation for our response. If there is a problem, it isn't Him. It's us. Justice. Kindness. Humility. That's all He wants.

God had given Israel all they needed to follow Him. But like Adam and Eve in the Garden, we would rather rule than be ruled. We would rather see ourselves as gods over the lives of others. We would rather put God in a tower or a box.

Though He is unrelenting, persistent, loving, faithful – God will be silent... for a while. But He is about to intervene in a new way. Consistent with His character of justice, mercy and humility, His pursuit of His people will bring complete renewal. The prophets know that God will not abandon them forever. They expect a Messiah to come and restore the land to Israel. His name will be great: a military commander, a priest, a king.

They have big expectations. Do you?

Ponder

Isaiah 9:2–7

Questions to Consider

If you've been waiting for God to act in your life, is there something you could do in the meanwhile? How can you show justice? Love mercy? Walk humbly with God? In what ways should these qualities condition the expectations we might have of a messiah?

Closing Prayer

Lord, too often I expect the wrong things of You. Remind me of Your character and show me who You are. Condition my expectations of You and myself, and help me to show justice, love mercy and walk humbly with You. Amen.

SESSION TWO

Unexpected Arrival

DAY 9
Wait for it...

Bible Reading
Luke 1:5–10

Daily Focus

In the song *You Want it Darker* by Leonard Cohen, released just before he died, he seems to put God on trial while recognising that He is still there. There is a line that conjures up an image of expectant hope that is irreversibly dashed as he sings of 'a million candles burning for the help that never came.' Candles are lit in churches and cathedrals in the hope that God will hear the desperate prayers of believers. Sometimes we might feel that we have lit many candles for help that does not seem to come. If we hang on to our belief at all, it is a hope against hope.

The prophets surveyed the devastation of the landscape and the persistent behaviour of God's people who flaunted His law and belied His character of love and justice. In the pattern of running away from Him and God chasing after them to bring them back home, perhaps the Israelites wondered if it would be this way forever. Always moving, never arriving. Always waiting, never achieving. The idea that God would bring lasting peace – was this just a dream?

For some, it was a dream worth pursuing, even when God was silent. Zechariah and his wife lived blamelessly, following all of the commandments and regulations of God. You'd expect that God might reward them for their faithfulness and answer their prayers for a child. But He hadn't. Still they didn't give up serving Him. God cannot be bargained with like that. *Do what I want or I won't worship You* is not an option for a faithful servant of the Most High.

As a priest, Zechariah was simply faithful to his role as intercessor for the people. Whether God spoke or was silent was not his responsibility. His job was to assist the prayers of the people by offering incense at the altar while they prayed outside. He wouldn't do this task often, but when the lot fell to him, he would enter the sanctuary and do what many had done before. He went even though it seemed scary; even though nothing dramatic ever seemed to happen. He went even though he had no expectation that God would speak.

We don't go to church to get away from the world but to bring the needs of the world to God. Sometimes – many times – it might seem like He doesn't hear the cry He invites us to bring. We light the candles and burn the incense. We sing the songs and pray the prayers. But we hear nothing.

In a culture of instant gratification where everything happens now, we get frustrated if there is a two-second delay in a website loading. Advent turns all of that on its head. The world moves so fast that we feel we are spinning out of control, and the packed agenda of Christmas seems to add to that. But this is a time to wait. To be quiet. To listen. Even when we don't expect Him to speak.

Ponder

Isaiah 40:27–31

Questions to Consider

How do you hold on to hope when God seems to be silent? How can you find silent spaces to listen for God even when everything is so busy?

Closing Prayer

Lord, I wait for You in the silence. Help me to listen. Be with me in the silence even when I'm not expecting You to speak. Give me patience to wait on Your timing, especially when it doesn't match my own. Amen.

DAY 10

Unexpected silence

Bible Reading

Luke 1:11–17

Daily Focus

It's often at the moment of greatest silence that our expectations are blown to pieces. That's certainly what happened for Zechariah. As he enters the sanctuary, he sees an angel standing near the altar. Understandably, he is terrified. (It wasn't often that a priest would see a vision or encounter an angelic being.) The angel tells him: 'your prayer has been heard. Your wife Elizabeth will bear you a son' (v13).

We often think that this is an answer to Zechariah's personal prayer for a child. But remember all those people praying outside? Remember the reason Zechariah went into the sanctuary in the first place? It was to bring before God the prayers of the people for the consolation of Israel. The prayer that God heard wasn't simply the prayer of Zechariah's heart: it was the prayer of His people for their redemption. Zechariah gets to be part of this new, unexpected development in God's story. The angel tells him that his son will turn many hearts to God; he will be a prophet who will prepare people for the Lord. This isn't just an answer to an individual prayer. This is big. This is a game-changer. This is totally unexpected.

The unexpected is sometimes hard to believe. So it was for Zechariah. Even though the angel Gabriel gave him this very specific message, he doubted its truth. His eyes turned immediately to the obstacles rather than the promise. *I'm old. My wife is old. How do I know any of this is true?* It becomes clear that the only way the people will accept this amazing news is by preventing Zechariah from voicing any more concerns about God's mission. Gabriel tells Zechariah that he will now be unable to speak until the promise has come to pass, and Elizabeth gives birth to a son named John.

If we feel that the Church has no message of hope for the world today, perhaps we too need to ask ourselves if we have been unbelieving in the face of God's promise. Too often we interject our own agendas onto God's plans. Engaging with His mission is too often focused on us, our limitations, and not on what God has clearly given to us to do. When God has given us the greatest news of all to share, are we sometimes silent?

Maybe God hasn't been silent after all. Maybe we are. When we doubt that God can accomplish the unexpected – like Zechariah did – we have nothing to say.

Ponder
Isaiah 6

Questions to Consider
What have been your moments of greatest doubt in accepting God's promise? In what ways do we expect individual prayers to be answered but miss the big picture where God is also at work? What does it look like when God answers the prayers of an entire community?

Closing Prayer
Lord, forgive me when my faith is so small that I struggle to believe Your promises. Help me not to dampen the message of Your good news with my own doubts. Give me eyes to see and ears to hear what You want to do in my life and in Your world. Amen.

DAY 11

Elizabeth and Mary

Bible Reading

Luke 1:39–56

Daily Focus

Zechariah may have been silenced but, in the unfolding Christmas story, the women are heard. This is noteworthy, considering the patriarchal society they lived in and how rarely women in Scripture are quoted. To be a woman in those days was to be regarded as barely human. But the Bible gives voice to those who bear the image of God – male and female. Leading up to Jesus' birth, those who were outside of society are included. Those who were far away are brought near.

In this case, we can see that Zechariah's silence is turning normal hierarchy on its head. The religious establishment, which Zechariah represents, has nothing to say, while the excluded and humble sing loud songs of praise. Mary's song isn't just about abstract ideas; her song is a description of what is unfolding in their midst. The powerful are brought low, and the lowly are raised up.

In this priestly silence, we hear Elizabeth, who is the first to publicly reveal the identity of the baby that Mary is carrying. As John leaps in Elizabeth's womb, she is led to understand that something amazing is happening and contrasts Mary's belief with Zechariah's unbelief. 'Blessed is she who has believed that the Lord would fulfil his promises to her!' (v45).

Zechariah's disbelief of the Lord's promise was followed by his enforced silence. Mary's belief is followed by her free song of praise. Zechariah's tongue was tied; Mary's voice is released. Her song rides on the wind and echoes down through the generations. It describes exactly what she is experiencing. She embraces the call of God on her life; she rejoices that He has looked on her with favour. Under His strength, He puts the prideful in their place. The hungry are filled and the rich are sent away empty. And in all of this, He has remembered His people. He has never let them go. 'He has helped his servant Israel, and remembered to be merciful. For he made this promise to our ancestors, to Abraham and to his children forever' (vv54–55, NLT).

Mary's Magnificat – the longest passage spoken by a woman in the New Testament – speaks not of calm or longing or introspection. (People who struggle daily for survival have no such reflective luxury.) Instead we have the raw, contextual proclamation of justice for the hungry and powerless. We have a testimony of God's favour with Mary who is neither wealthy nor powerful nor male. We have an urgently unfolding story that demonstrates something very unexpected is happening. Zechariah's tongue will eventually be released, and he will prophesy powerfully about Jesus when John is born. But today is Elizabeth's day. Today is Mary's day. Today, they sing.

Ponder
Exodus 15:20–21

Questions to Consider
Have you ever been in a gathering with something to say but you were overlooked, and no one would listen? How did that feel? How does it feel when your voice is heard *and* received? Can you think of others without a voice that you need to listen to?

Closing Prayer
Lord, help me to hear the song of the voiceless. If it's mine, let me sing. If it's another, let me listen. Help me to lift the songs of real life to You. Help us to make room for everyone's voice in Your community. Amen.

DAY 12

Who notices the unexpected?

Bible Reading
Luke 2:1–7

Daily Focus

In the Christmas season, we might grow a little weary of the sentimentality we sometimes encounter in our churches and other venues. Lovely as they are, beyond the children's nativity play is a faith that can make a difference in the harsh reality of the darkest nights and most anguished days.

As we properly examine the nativity story, we discover a slightly different picture of the first Christmas than what we usually encounter on Christmas cards. To begin with, the word often translated as 'inn' (v7, KJV) is more accurately translated as 'guest room' (NIV). We can be confident from archeology that in a typical first-century home in Palestine there would be the main living quarters, the sleeping quarters (including a guest room) and the storeroom with space for animals. Because of the census, the guest room in the home of Joseph's relatives was occupied. But the family may have cleared out the space normally occupied by the animals and allowed Mary and Joseph to stay there.

God-made-flesh came into the world not in a quiet rustic barn, but in the midst of a bustling home in a heaving town. Right at the centre of human reality and the daily struggles of life, Jesus is born, God with us. In the middle of the chaos, the mess, the laughter, the noise, the complexity, God is here.

Even though it's likely that Jesus was born in a family home rather than a wooden stable, let's not imagine a nice bungalow in a middle-class neighbourhood. Living standards in ancient Palestine were not quite like the comparitively palatial comforts we may have come to enjoy. We can't really imagine what it was like for a very young woman without education and little experience of life to give birth without her own family nearby and without medical support. She and her baby would soon be on the run, and the blood of innocent children would cover the land. None of this is reflected in the nativity set on my mantlepiece.

God has always noticed the overlooked. He has never been influenced by worldly prejudices, but has always been with the weak and the poor, lifting them up and reminding them that He is with them. 'God chose the foolish things of the world to shame the wise; God chose the weak things of the world to shame the strong' (1 Cor. 1:27).

Many people had given up waiting for a messiah. They were comfortable in their lives and did not want to be disturbed. Those who were looking for Him expected a king, a military ruler, a religious leader, a person of wealth and power. Someone who would take their side and give them a political advantage.

They didn't expect this. A baby in a manger, in a family home, in a town crowded with busy people.

If we think that Jesus is not relevant to our lives, it's very easy to miss Him at Christmas. The question for us this Advent is not perhaps that of the nativity-play innkeeper: *Will we make room for Jesus?* The question is: *As He shows up in our busy and distracted lives, will we notice Him at all?*

Ponder
1 Corinthians 1:18–31

Questions for Reflection
Why do you think we can so easily miss Jesus in our midst at Christmastime? Where do you see God at work today?

Closing Prayer
Lord God, help me to notice Jesus. In the busyness, in the worry, in the celebrations, in the conflicts, I want to notice Him at work around me. Help me to notice. Help me to follow. Amen.

DAY 13

The shepherds noticed

Bible Reading
Luke 2:8–20

Daily Focus

The night that forever changed the course of history went by largely unnoticed. For most people, it was hardly remarkable that a young woman should give birth in a busy town, where families had gathered for the census. It may have been an inconvenience – another room crowded, another baby crying. But we know little of what happened in the room that night, other than the fact that a baby was born who would change everything.

What was hidden at first from the powerful was instead revealed to those on the margins of society. No telegrams turned up at the palace of the king or at the homes of the priests. What we are told is that messengers from God Himself were sent, but not to the halls of the wealthy. Instead, on a hillside, in the dark of the night, the angels appeared to tell the most amazing news... to a group of shepherds. The shepherds noticed what happened that night. In fact, they had little choice.

The angels, shining with the glory of God, announced to them that a saviour – the Messiah – was born. They told the shepherds where they could find the baby, and gave a heavenly performance of praise. All of this affirms the favour the shepherds had found with God: that He should reveal the light of salvation to them in the dark of the night.

The shepherds had little option but to take in this amazing sight and news – but they were not required to *believe*. Nevertheless, they made haste to Bethlehem, the busy town where the baby was, and they found what they were looking for. As they excitedly told the story of what had happened, people started to buzz. They started to take notice.

It is interesting to consider who was *not* among the first to be told about the birth of a saviour. The priests – the Pharisees in particular –

might have been watching for a sign but were too caught up in their rules and regulations to imagine that God's promise might be fulfilled in their lifetime. Those who should have been spiritual shepherds to the people were overlooked in favour of real shepherds. The good news was for those who cared for the flock, rather than those who exploited the flock.

Throughout the narrative of Jesus' birth, it becomes clear who is among the first to find favour in God's eyes: the poor and the worn-out. A saviour has come, bringing hope to the weary. He lifts up the oppressed. He gives Mary something to think about and the shepherds something to be excited about.

If you feel overlooked and unnoticed this Advent, if you feel left aside or left behind, listen to the song of the angels. In the dark of your night, they announce that a saviour has been born for you, born for those who know they haven't got it all together, to give you joy and peace.

Once again, the unexpected takes centre stage. Unexpected Jesus.

Ponder

Luke 15:1–7

Questions to Consider

Why do you think the good news of Jesus was announced first to the shepherds and not to the religious leaders? What does it mean for us today that Jesus seemed to favour those on the margins of society?

Closing Prayer

Thank You, Lord, that You did not reveal Yourself first to the powerful but to the lowly. Thank You for including the shepherds in the celebration of Jesus' birth. Thank You for including me. Amen.

DAY 14

The wise ones noticed

Bible Reading

Matthew 2:1–12

Daily Focus

In Matthew's account of the birth of Jesus, another piece of the story is revealed. An angel has appeared to Joseph to tell him what's going to take place in his family, and he is told that people will call the baby 'Emmanuel' meaning 'God with us'. The God who has chased after His people and never let them go is now with them in flesh and blood and bones.

The shepherds were not the only ones to witness heavenly signs. People of means and privilege also noticed that something had happened that was worthy of their attention. The magi from the east saw signs in the heavens and made their way to worship the child.

Their decision to travel would not have been taken lightly. They would have to find the sign in the stars that signified to them that a king had been born. They would have discussed among themselves its meaning, and decided that it was no ordinary, local figure, but one of cosmic significance. They would have packed their things, some carefully chosen gifts and travelled a long distance to finally see Jesus. It would be some time before they actually got there.

We know little about these learned people; we are usually more informed by popular fictional representations of the wise men. The Bible doesn't tell us exactly who they are. In fact, we cannot say with certainty how many there were, or whether all of them were men. Indeed, the passage may remind us of the visit of the Queen of Sheba to Solomon (1 Kings 10). What is clear is that these visitors were wealthy and they were foreigners. Could they expect a welcome?

Matthew's Gospel is known to be influenced by the book of Isaiah. In Isaiah, the people of Israel are reminded that they are a chosen people not only for their own good, but in order to be a light to the nations (Isa. 49:6-7). By neglecting justice and mercy, the Israelites had inhibited their witness to others. With the birth of Jesus, however, the door is open wide and the light shines once again to all the nations. Those who were thought to be far away, those who were outsiders, are brought near.

These visitors from a foreign land are welcomed. Their gifts are accepted. Their worship is received. They are included in what God is doing. God's selection of a chosen people was never meant to be exclusive. Rather, it was to be a starting place from where all the world would know that He is God. Where all would be called to come and worship the newborn King – God with us.

God is once again walking in His garden. And all creation is invited to join Him.

Ponder

Genesis 12:1–3

Questions to Consider

Why is the visit of the magi important for understanding the significance of Jesus' birth beyond Israel? How do we respond to 'outsiders' who come to church at Christmastime? How do we welcome those from different ethnicities and social backgrounds into the local family of God?

Closing Prayer

Thank You, Lord, that this good news is for *all* the world. Help us to offer a wide embrace to everyone who will gather for worship this Christmas, even if this is the only time we see them. Teach us to welcome everybody with the love of Christ. Amen.

DAY 15
Herod noticed

Bible Reading
Matthew 2:13–23

Daily Focus
If the powerful didn't notice Jesus at first, it wouldn't take them long to realise that there was a new ruler in town. Alerted by the visit from the eastern magi, Herod the king perceived a threat to his rule. Of course, the magi, looking for a king, assumed the best place to start looking was at a king's palace. But when they didn't find the child there, they kept seeking until they did. Once they had and 'bowed down and worshipped him' (v11), they returned home without reporting to Herod. So Herod was still in the dark about where this new king was. Jesus was found in such an unlikely place that Herod figured the only way to be sure of getting rid of the child was to order the killing of all children under two years old.

Imagine someone so afraid of losing their power that they would murder thousands of little children to protect themselves. We don't have to think too hard to come up with contemporary parallels. All the world over, halls of power are filled with people who are self-interested, self-protecting and terrified that someone may come and take what they feel is rightly theirs.

Those of us who live in the western world might even see this pattern reflected in our own lives in some way. *This country is my country. I have earned what I have. It's mine to protect.* When strangers show up, we may be concerned that our position might somehow be compromised and that our privileges will be taken away. This isn't the way of the kingdom of God.

In humility, we are to consider others better than ourselves. We are to look to the interests of others, and away from our own selfish ambitions. This is the way of Jesus Christ, who 'being in very nature God, did not consider equality with God something to be used to his own advantage; rather, he made himself nothing by taking the very nature of a servant, being made in human likeness' (Phil. 2:6–7).

And so we see a young family on the run from tyranny and violence. They head to Egypt and are spared the worst: the murder of young children in and around Bethlehem. Prideful rebellion against God continues to wreak havoc on creation. In the world, the powerful continue to hold sway.

Those who fear losing their own power shore up their defenses by visiting fear on others. But in a world of pain, conflict and sorrow, Jesus is on the run with the refugees. That's where God-in-the-flesh has chosen to be. The wails of mothers whose babies are torn from their arms in the night, the laments of those who will no longer nurse their infants, and the eerie quiet that creeps in as the sounds of play fall silent, all rise before God's eternal throne. The Christmas story is as real as the terror of war, the horror of abuse, the loneliness of oppression and the darkness of death.

Herod seems to be in control. But soon he will be dead. And Jesus will return.

Ponder
Philippians 2:1–18

Questions to Consider
How do you respond as a Christian to the tyrannical abuse of power by some leaders in the world today? Have there been dark times in your life when it was hard to hold on to your faith? What helped you through?

Closing Prayer
God, You are the one to whom all earthly powers are subject. Though I do not understand why so many suffer at the hands of evil rulers, I trust that You will hold them to account. Help me to be Your hands and feet to those who are hurting in the world today. Amen.

DAY 16

Anna and Simeon noticed

Bible Reading
Luke 2:22–38

Daily Focus

Remember those people praying outside the Temple when Zechariah went to the altar? They were seeking the consolation of Israel, and the angel told Zechariah that his prayer on their behalf had been answered. What then unfolded – a baby born in a humble stable – was hardly what anyone was expecting.

Many months later, we visit the Temple again, and meet two of those people who were praying for a messiah. Simeon and Anna had been waiting for a long time, and were now quite old, particularly by the standards of the time. Their persistence in hope, and in not surrendering their expectations in the face of a very long wait, is finally rewarded. And their prize is that they are given an opportunity to prophecy and rejoice at seeing their expectations fulfilled.

Simeon blesses the child and His parents – especially Mary. But there is a barb in the prophecy. The child will bring salvation, but He will be opposed by many. 'And a sword will pierce your own heart too' (v35). We can imagine Mary's countenance turning from delight to distress. *What does this mean? What will happen to my child? What pain am I going to face?* This isn't the sort of message a new mother would expect to hear.

In our churches, we can often be dismissive of older voices, accusing them of being stuck in the past and out of touch, but those with wisdom of experience are sometimes able to identify God at work. Maybe those who have time to pray and think are most ready to see what God is doing. Perhaps they can see what others miss.

Just as Simeon is finishing his words to the family, Anna approaches them with her own words of prophecy. A woman of great age, and great devotion to God, she too sees something special in Jesus. She praises God and speaks about Jesus to those expecting God to show up and do something for His people.

Even though Simeon's prophecy and Anna's thanksgiving were uttered with joyful praise, the whole encounter would have been overwhelming for Mary and Joseph. They knew that Jesus was no ordinary child and must have been concerned about what the road ahead would look like. As they prepared for an unusual future for their son, they would also need to prepare their hearts for breaking. The sacrifice of their son would be a sacrifice for them too.

Ponder

Hebrews 11:8–12

Questions to Consider

In what ways are the voices of the elderly heard or neglected in our churches today? Who are some of the elders who speak wisdom into your own life? In what ways has life with Jesus been difficult for you?

Closing Prayer

Jesus, I sometimes find it hard to walk with You when the way is not easy. Give me courage for the journey and companions for the way. Help me to hear the wisdom of those who have been this way before. Amen.

SESSION THREE

Unexpected Encounters

DAY 17

Preparing the way

Bible Reading
John 1:1–34

Daily Focus
John the Baptist had known Jesus for a long time – since before birth. As they grew up, they probably met regularly and got to know one another. In today's reading, they are now both grown men and John's ministry of repentance is in full swing. John has caused enough commotion in Jerusalem to attract the attention of the religious folks who ask him about the Messiah.

John is clear from the outset about his own identity. He is *not* the light; he gives testimony to the light. He is *not* the Messiah, but he is preparing the way for the Messiah. They should watch and wait. While the visitors from Jerusalem are still hanging around, John looks up and sees his cousin. 'Look, the Lamb of God, who takes away the sin of the world!' (v29). John makes it clear to his followers that he believes Jesus to be the Son of God.

The revelation that his own cousin, a local Galilean, is the 'Lamb of God' is probably a surprise for John too. He points to Jesus' baptism as the point when he knew Jesus was more than a relative or friend. That was when he saw the Spirit descend like a dove, and he knew that it would be Jesus who would baptise with the Holy Spirit.

Later, however, John has some doubts. Just as Jesus' ministry is drawing crowds, John sends some of his followers to ask an unexpected question: 'Are you the one who is to come, or should we expect someone else?' (Luke 7:19). John – who had first recognised the Messiah in His mother's womb, who had baptised Jesus and saw the Spirit rest on Him like a dove, who had declared, 'Look, the Lamb of God, who takes away the sins of the world' (v29) – is still not sure that Jesus is what he expected a messiah to be. *Maybe He isn't all that I thought. Maybe He is just my cousin. Maybe I got it wrong.*

Jesus sends an encouraging message back to His cousin: 'Go back and report to John what you have seen and heard: the blind receive sight, the lame walk... the dead are raised and the good news is proclaimed to the poor' (Luke 7:22). The fulfilment of the prophetic expectation is met in Jesus' ministry, which John will understand.

Jesus doesn't always do what we expect Him to. We can be prone to questions or even doubt. We can oscillate between passionate conviction and wavering scepticism. At times like this it's important to consider the evidence and remember how Jesus is a clear fulfilment of prophetic expectation in Scripture. However, if John the Baptist had wobbly moments, we might expect to have them too sometimes. Thankfully, Jesus speaks kindly. He points to the evidence beyond expectation. He reveals that in the kingdom of God, the unbelieving religious leaders are out, and the weak, the lame and the poor are in. Even John didn't expect that.

Ponder
Luke 4:16–24

Questions to Consider
Why do you think John was unsure that Jesus was the Messiah, after making his previous declaration that Jesus was the 'Lamb of God'? How did the Pharisees respond to John's declaration about Jesus? What things have caused you to doubt Jesus' identity?

Closing Prayer
Forgive me when I doubt You, Lord. Remind me of how You meet the expectations of the prophets, even if You don't meet mine. Thank You for confronting my doubt with reassurance and not judgment. Amen.

DAY 18

Betrayed by the reality?

Bible Reading

Matthew 23:1–36

Daily Focus

So much for 'Gentle Jesus, meek and mild'. In today's reading, Jesus is unexpectantly hard, confronting and exacting. With strong terms, He is exposing the hypocrisy of the priests and letting them know that they are a bit like expensive coffins: impressive on the outside, but completely dead on the inside. He is making clear that it's not only what we do that's important, it's about our very being.

The Pharisees didn't just wake up one day and invent a system that would crush the people who were unable to live up to legalistic demands. They didn't think at all that they were leading God's flock away from His gentle shepherding. They thought they were being faithful. But action by action, the image they wished to portray as godly leaders was betrayed by the reality. They found themselves so far away from God's agenda that they were leading people astray.

Action by action, we build our character. Whether in public or in private, what we do is both a revelation and a construction of who we are. In a media-rich world, there seems to be a feeling that we can hide behind the illusion of anonymity and be different people in different places and times. We think our actions are without consequence.

For the Pharisees, the inside failed to match the outside. It can be the same for us. We might hide behind invented online identities – one image on Instagram, another on Facebook, another on TikTok. Maybe we even invent a secret identity on a dubious platform. We needn't tell anyone. Nobody knows us there. It's as though we are free to do whatever we wish so long as nobody sees us, and our real identity is hidden.

The notion of a world free of responsibility, free of consequences doesn't square with the best of human reasoning, let alone with a Christian understanding of ethics.

In one of Aesop's fable, the birds are warned by the swallow to eat the hemp seeds before the seeds grow up into plants that are woven into nets that will be used to catch them. Destroy the seeds of destruction or they will destroy you. This is what happened to the Pharisees. When Jesus encountered them, He wasn't meeting some religious folks who had simply made a mistake. He was confronting leaders who had time and time again resisted the Spirit of God, and instead devised their own religion rather than lead people to true worship. This isn't just a failure of ethics, it's a failure in the formation of a character, and the denial of a God-given responsibility to nurture, and not crush, the weak.

Following Christ, especially as leaders, is not about recognition and veneration. It's not about impressing people with how holy you are and forcing others to follow the laws you lay down. It's about daily taking up your cross, dying to yourself, your desires, what you want – and pouring out your life in service to others.

Ponder
Ezekiel 34:1–10

Questions to Consider
How consistent are your actions with your beliefs? Could there be some ways in which you are (consciously or unconsciously) making it difficult for people to come to faith in Jesus? How can you make it easier?

Closing Prayer
Jesus, You showed how You cared for the weak and the poor. Give me a heart for humble service. Help me to be a bridge to faith for others and not a barrier. Amen.

DAY 19

What happens next

Bible Reading

Luke 5:1–7

Daily Focus

There are many interesting encounters between Jesus and Peter recorded in Scripture, but few are as unexpected as this one on the sea of Galilee. In small stone houses dwelled people who made a living from the land and the sea. Rather than being lowly and uneducated, fishermen were actually some of the wealthiest businessmen in the area. Together they worked the boats and caught the fish that fed their communities, and provided income for their families, probably for generations. They didn't know anything else. Then along comes a man who changes everything – not in a day, but in a moment.

Peter was clearly worn out. Possibly bored and fed up, he'd been fishing all night with no result. He figured that he might as well let the local celebrity take his boat for a while, and he hands it over, so that Jesus can teach a little way out from shore. At least it provides some entertainment and distraction while he cleans his nets. *Meh. The world is all a bit 'samey'. A bit uninteresting. What could possibly change things?*

'Put out into deep water, and let down the nets for a catch,' Jesus tells him. Peter protests. He really doesn't want to go out there again. He knows the score and he's seen it all before. Jesus persists, and Peter relents. They go out and let the nets down again. From here, you know what happens. The catch is bigger than ever.

If you're anything like me, you've heard this taught and preached countless times. We might even be a bit 'meh' about the whole thing ourselves. *Yes, yes, Jesus brought a miraculous catch of fish. Great. Yes, I know, we need to have the courage to let the nets down one more time.* But is the message *really* just about doing what Jesus says? If we look closely, the pinnacle of the story is not Peter letting down the nets. It's what happens next. It's the unexpected act of Jesus as Lord of all nature, supernaturally filling the nets with fish until they break.

It's not what Peter did. It's what the Lord did despite Peter's initial reluctance. It's about what God does when we are at our worst, when we care little, when we are tired and worn out. At those times, let's lower the nets one more time, not because there's some sort of magic in it, but because we might see God do something incredible.

Ponder
Matthew 11:28–30

Questions to Consider
When do you feel a bit 'meh' about your Christian walk? What is it like when you get bored or tired of your faith? What sort of miracle would change your attitude? What would it look like for a big catch of fish to turn up in your life today?

Closing Prayer
Jesus, forgive me when I lose focus and my commitment is weak. Remind me who You are and what You can do. I long to see people come into Your kingdom. Help me to let down the nets when You say so. Amen.

DAY 20
Leaving it all behind

Bible Reading
Luke 5:8–11

Daily Focus

Yesterday we read about an unexpected catch of fish – an outcome that was surprising considering Peter's lack of enthusiasm. Glimpsing at what God can do (even when we are at our worst) is still not the most unexpected part of this story.

Peter's reaction to the miraculous catch of fish is one of repentance. He realises that his expectations were too low, but Jesus did something amazing even when his faith was small. The miraculous catch of fish told Peter who Jesus really was, changing his heart, his expectations and his whole future. The one who had the power over nature to bring a catch of fish like that would have the power to command Peter's devotion. The full nets were not a blessing on Peter's current occupation, but a sign that his occupation was about to change. Jesus then said, 'follow me' (Matt. 4:19). Without the catch of fish, Peter would not have known with whom he was speaking. But now it's clear, and he can't help but follow.

Peter and his business partners left their boats. We are not talking here about a plastic kayak, good for a weekend paddle: the boats were their livelihoods. Their boats were their identity. The boats were who they had been for generations. His family must have worried and wondered, *If Peter follows this man, who is going to feed us? How can he leave his boat? How will we live?* Peter saw that the one who filled the nets miraculously was not only worthy of devotion but was also able to feed his family and the community.

Peter and the others with him stood on the lakeshore and took one last long look at the boats. The most familiar things in the world. The only world they knew. And they turned away and followed Jesus. Nobody expected that.

We too are invited to leave our boats and follow Jesus. But there might be things we find difficult to leave behind; things that we are attached to; things that form our sense of identity; things that are worthy in themselves but not what God has given to us to do. To us, Jesus says, 'Don't be afraid; from now on you will fish for people' (v10).

Ponder

Luke 9:23–27

Questions to Consider

What most shapes your identity? What's your boat – the thing that keeps you busy, but also keeps you from following Jesus more fully? Why is it difficult to leave it behind?

Closing Prayer

Lord, I know You are able to do more than I could ask or imagine. Help me to recognise the things in my life that keep me from following You more closely. Give me courage to trust that Your grace is sufficient for each day. Renew in me the joy of work for Your kingdom. Amen.

DAY 21

Worthy of the gift

Bible Reading

John 4:1–26

Daily Focus

The meeting of Jesus and the Samaritan woman is one perhaps of the most unexpected in all of the Gospels.

Jesus is travelling through Samaria and, in the heat of the day, He stops at Jacob's well for some refreshment. His disciples have gone into town for food, and there is nobody else there except for a Samaritan woman. In those days, not only were women marginalised, but Samaritans and Jews were known for their mutual hatred of one another. The woman certainly did not expect to hear Jesus ask her for a drink, but He did. Recovering from the shock, she finds her voice and challenges Him about how He can speak with her. The conversation turns towards the subject of water and the water that Jesus gives, which won't just sit in a well but will flow like a river. She takes Him on. 'Sir, give me this water so I won't get thirsty again and have to keep coming here to draw water' (v15).

Jesus then becomes personal and tells the woman to fetch her husband. '"I have no husband," she replied' (v17). With deep insight into her life, He agrees. 'The fact is you have had five husbands, and the man you have now is not your husband' (v18). Seeing that He is a prophet, she deflects His insight and engages in a discussion about religion. Finally, she gives up, and tells Him that the Messiah will sort out all disagreements between Samaritans and Jews.

I am He. That's me. The one speaking to you. I am the Messiah.

Her life is transformed in a moment – and not just because she has found forgiveness for her past. She is transformed because her dignity is restored. She is a human being loved by God.

We can reasonably assume that the Samaritan woman was an outcast of society because she had likely been abused by men all her life. In that cultural context, women were completely dependent on men for survival. A man could dispose of a woman pretty easily. It's probable that this woman had been passed from man to man five times with very little choice. She was no doubt abused, learning to scrape by on a bare existence in between relationships. And now, in desperation for survival, she is with a man who perhaps refuses to marry her. She is the lowest of the low of society.

The most unexpected thing is that Jesus doesn't just forgive the woman, He liberates her. He shows her that she's worth so much more than her husbands have led her to believe. He shows her that she is worthy of the attention of a prophet, the very presence of the Messiah. She is not only worthy to give Him a drink, but she is worthy of His gift of living water. She is a deeply loved human being.

Ponder

John 7:37–39

Questions to Consider

When have you felt like an outsider or that you don't belong? What helps you to feel included in a group? How can you help those who are often at the margins to feel included?

Closing Prayer

Forgive me, Lord, when I judge others according to standards that I cannot live up to myself. Remind me that they are deeply loved by You. Help me to show Your love and acceptance. Amen.

DAY 22

From outcast to evangelist

Bible Reading

John 4:27–41

Daily Focus

When the disciples return and see Jesus speaking to the woman, none of them say a word. They don't challenge Jesus, asking Him why He is talking with *her*. This alone raises the woman's dignity. While she's with Jesus, she is safe. She doesn't have to defend herself or feel crushed. Jesus has given her a glimpse of what it's like to be a woman respected and respectable. He helps her to see herself as He sees her. And when she gets a glimpse of her dignity again, her head is held just a little bit higher.

The woman leaves her shame, her fear, her abuse, her oppression behind. She leaves her water jar behind. She doesn't need it anymore. She has the living water that Jesus was talking about. The old has gone and the new has come. She runs back to town and excitedly tells everyone to 'Come, see a man who told me everything I've ever done' (v29). Clearly the transformation has made an impact because people listen to her. They *do* come and see. And they come to believe.

Like the best of evangelists, the Samaritan woman doesn't just tell her story. She invites people to come and meet Jesus for themselves. The one who has made such a difference to her might make a difference to them too. And He does. They hear for themselves and come to believe that Jesus is the Saviour of the world.

If you have been a victim of structural systems or cultural attitudes that have discriminated against you and held you down, you are not disqualified from receiving living water. You too are invited to leave your jar, receive living water and let it spill over to those around you. He sends you to invite people to come and see.

However, perhaps we have also been those who have held others down with our judgments and scrutiny. Who do we routinely exclude because we fail to recognise their dignity as bearers of the image of God? What would their lives look like if we saw them as Christ sees them, and not with our own eyes? We are invited to leave the gossip of the water cooler and instead be filled with the living water. As Jesus fills us up, He sends us out. Let's splash it everywhere – there's a world of people in need of refreshment.

Ponder
2 Corinthians 5:16–20

Questions to Consider
What walls have you built around your family, church or community group? Are there certain people you don't want anything to do with? Are there people who don't want anything to do with *you*? In what ways do you need to be liberated in your life? How can you help others to know freedom in Christ?

Closing Prayer
Jesus, I celebrate that Your good news is for everybody, even me. Thank You that You break down walls of rejection and repair relationships that need healing. Help me to accept myself as You do. Send me on Your mission to invite others to 'come and see' that You are the Saviour of the world. Amen.

DAY 23

Something better

Bible Reading

Mark 10:17–31

Daily Focus

Peter left his boat behind. The Samaritan woman left her jar behind. The rich young man left Jesus behind.

In another unexpected encounter, a young man wants to know from Jesus what he is required to do to inherit eternal life. Jesus tells him to keep the commandments and reels off several as examples. Notice how Jesus only lists the second half of the Ten Commandments, relating to our ethical behaviour with one another. (The first five relate to our worship and devotion to God.) Jesus mentions the latter ones for a reason: He knows that the young man has tried to live a good life.

The young man assures Jesus that he has kept these commandments since childhood. Jesus looks at him not with judgment, but with love. He tells the man that he lacks one thing: he must give his money to the poor and come follow Jesus. The young man lived an ethical life, but he struggled to put God first. The first five commandments were neglected, starting with the first: 'You shall have no other gods before me' (Exod. 20:3). The money was his boat. The money was his jar.

If Peter didn't leave the boat, he'd never know what it was to fish for people. If the Samaritan woman never left her jar, she'd never taste the living water. If the young man didn't leave his wealth, he wouldn't know the richness of the kingdom of God. Each had the chance to find something better than they could imagine. But the young man couldn't fathom what life would be like without wealth and the privileges it brought. What could be better than what he had? The man went away sad. He would never know. While Peter got something better than what he left, and the Samaritan woman got so much more than what she had come for, the rich young man didn't get to find out what would be of far greater value than what he had.

In today's reading, Peter reminds Jesus that he and the other disciples had given up everything they knew to follow Jesus (v28). The Lord does not rebuke them. Rather, He assures them that what they have given up for the sake of the good news, they will one day receive back in full. But what is seen as first place in this world will be turned on its head in the kingdom of God. The 'first will be last, and the last first' (v31).

What do we desire in our lives that is greater than our love for God? Is it possible that we are missing out on a harvest of people, the water of life and the eternity of the kingdom because we are afraid to let go of our security? This can happen to individuals and to churches. To let go is to take a risk. I wonder how many times we miss out on the blessing God has for us because we are unwilling to give up security, stability, success, control or whatever it is that we desire more than God. We may find that desire difficult to acknowledge, let alone surrender. If we are used to being first, why would we want to be last?

Ponder
Matthew 6:19–21

Questions to Consider
Is there something in your life that hinders your relationship with God? What have you given up in order to follow Jesus?

Closing Prayer
Lord, I confess that I often want to be first. Nobody really wants to be last. Give me courage to surrender the things I cling to most, and to serve You above all. Amen.

DAY 24

Seeing, and seen

Bible Reading

Luke 19:1–10

Daily Focus

Zacchaeus, whose short stature perhaps reminds us of the children who came to Jesus in the previous chapter, climbs a tree. He's giving it all he's got to catch a glimpse of Jesus but the crowd is pressing in and he can't see. We are reminded of Jesus' words to His disciples not to hinder those who want to come to Him. Clearly somebody, somewhere, has already told Zacchaeus something about Jesus or he wouldn't be so keen to see Him. Somewhere, somebody has sown a seed. But just like the disciples tried to prevent the children from seeing Jesus, so this crowd is in the way.

Often, we too are in the way, preventing others from seeing Jesus clearly. Instead of facilitating engagements with the Lord, we stand in the way with our own agendas and attitudes about who is in and who is out. Like the people in Jesus' day, we have our own expectations about who is included and who is excluded. Jesus constantly challenges expectations in unexpected ways.

Zacchaeus is definitely on the outside. He's not on the outside because he is short, but because he is a tax collector. Tax collectors were reviled people. But in the parable of the Pharisee and the tax collector (Luke 18:9–14), Jesus makes it clear that it is possible for tax collectors to be *more* righteous because they know that they have need of God than self-righteous folk who have not truly received God's grace and stand in the way of people's salvation.

While Zacchaeus was searching for Jesus, Jesus had searched him out and found him. Sometimes we strain hard to find God, without realising that God is pursuing us. But not only had Jesus found Zacchaeus, He elevated his status. Zacchaeus would not have been the local's choice for hosting the celebrity Jesus. But Jesus has chosen the unlikely one – so unlikely that one might be forgiven for wondering what Jesus is up to. Remember that in chapter 18 Jesus had reminded the disciples that it's hard for a rich person to enter the kingdom of heaven – and Zacchaeus is indeed rich. As a tax collector, it would be inevitable that some of his wealth was acquired in less-than-scrupulous ways. But with Jesus, anything is possible. He doesn't hit Zacchaeus over the head with teaching and moral demands. Instead, demonstrating the power of building relationships, He simply decides to share a meal with Zacchaeus. The fellowship of the table builds relationships. He declares that Zacchaeus – in contrast to the Pharisees – is a real son of Abraham. Now that's unexpected.

Over the next few days, you might be getting together with friends and family and sharing a meal. Perhaps there is someone who is on their own that you could invite to those celebrations. Follow Jesus' example and build relationships this Christmas.

Ponder
Matthew 9:9–13

Questions to Consider
In what ways have you experienced the Lord pursuing you in your life? In what ways have you tried to hide? When have you felt judged? What does it mean to you that Jesus might want to simply be with you, inviting you to spend time in His presence?

Closing Prayer
Lord, forgive me for drawing lines of who is in and who is out of Your kingdom. Forgive me for when I have counted others out, even myself. Thank You that You redraw the lines of inclusion. Help me not to be a barrier to Your kingdom agenda, but a host who welcomes guests at the door. Amen.

DAY 25

Into the light

Bible Reading

John 3:1–21

Daily Focus

We started this section with the Pharisees and how they rejected the message of Jesus. We ended up with Zacchaeus who, although a tax collector, was called a 'son of Abraham' by Jesus instead of the religious leaders who should have been the natural bearers of that title. Is there no hope for any of the Pharisees? Are all religious leaders bound to fail?

Enter Nicodemus – a Pharisee who we meet three times in the Gospel of John. The first time, he comes under the cover of darkness to meet with Jesus. He can't deny the miraculous signs he has seen, but he also can't reconcile the message of Jesus with the detailed religious practices he had been following so carefully in order to earn favour with God. Jesus tells Nicodemus that entering the kingdom of heaven is not about condemnation, but salvation; it's not about death, but life; it's not about darkness, but light. Jesus rejects the legalistic behavior of the Pharisees and shines a light on God's love. All of this turns Nicodemus' religion on its head. When Jesus challenges him to believe and be born again, however, Nicodemus is confused because the Pharisees had worked out so carefully what series of actions was required to be acceptable to God.

Sometimes we can be like Nicodemus. Despite our familiarity with the Bible, we can revert to religious observance to save us. We set up a system of rules that keep us in the dark and become oppressive to others. We need to find the courage to step out of the shadows, own our faith in the daylight and recognise that our religious practices do not earn God's favour. Eternal life is a gift from above.

The second time we meet Nicodemus is in John 7. Here he is defending Jesus to the Sanhedrin. Clearly his faith is developing and his courage is growing. By the time Jesus dies on the cross, Nicodemus has stepped fully into the light, bringing myrrh and aloes for Jesus's burial. He, who had first come under the cover of night, steps into the light of day with his faith in a big way.

It can be hard to come into the light. Squinting into the brightness means transforming our view of God, of ourselves and of the world. It means allowing Jesus to ask hard questions, and admitting that, in the light of day, our efforts at obedience are feebler and less impressive than we'd hoped. The message Jesus gives to Nicodemus of light, life and new birth is unexpected. We don't have to work our way to salvation. Jesus's love is given freely. The invitation to be born again frees us from thinking we can earn salvation by following rules and laws. Jesus comes not to condemn the world, but that the world, through Him, might be saved.

Surely the gift of life and light is my best gift of all. Today, Christmas Day, let's thank Jesus for bringing us out of darkness and into a glorious relationship with Him.

Ponder
John 8:12–20

Questions to Consider
Are there ways that you need to be 'born again' and follow Jesus with greater authenticity? What does it mean to you that Jesus came to love and not condemn the world?

Closing Prayer
Lord, teach me the joy and freedom of walking in the light with You. Give me the courage this Advent to step into the light of Christmas in a new way, embracing the love of God in Christ. Amen.

SESSION FOUR

Unexpected Return

DAY 26

We are the waiting

Bible Reading

Acts 1:1–11

Daily Focus

After all the disciples had given up in order to follow Jesus, the experience of the cross must have been completely devastating for them. But He did not leave them alone for long. At the peak of their desolation, He returned to them, raised to life again on the third day. Disbelief gave way to utter joy – *He's returned to us!*

Jesus' renewed presence lifted their spirits and hope returned. Sadly, some of their old ideas and thinking returned too. No matter how hard Jesus had tried to transform them in the past, their political agendas and personal ambitions came to the fore again. 'Lord, are you at this the time going to restore the kingdom to Israel?' (v6). They loved this idea, especially since it meant they might get to rule with Him. *You know, just a little golden throne on the side.* They thought something big was coming; their expectations were high.

But Jesus turns their idea on its head once again. They will receive power, but not of the political kind. *The Holy Spirit will come upon you and you will go on a mission. Here in Jerusalem, further afield, and to the places you despise. You have expectations of power and reward? I will surpass your expectations but it's not going to be easy. You're not only going to see a kingdom here but one that extends to the ends of the earth!* In other words, Jesus reorientates their expectations away from their desires, towards God's purposes.

By the time Jesus left the disciples to ascend to the Father, they had been through a rollercoaster of emotions and experiences. Their expectations of death and life had been turned completely upside-down – but they still didn't get it. Like us, they were slow to understand that

God's purposes don't always work according to our wants and desires. The exhilaration of encountering Jesus alive after they had lost all hope gives way to another round of bitter disappointment. *How can You go away? You've just come back to us – don't leave again!* No wonder they stood for so long, looking into the sky (Acts 1:11). *Wow! That's not what we expected. What now?* All they can do is wait.

Waiting is hard. It is the hardest part of expecting. Remember that special night out? That holiday you booked? Waiting for normal life to resume after lockdown? A short time can seem like forever when you're waiting for something significant. The Church too is in a period of waiting. During Advent, we remember not only the coming of Jesus to earth as a baby, we also recall His promise to return. This interim seems like a very long time. We get distracted by our own agendas and expectations. We make our demands of what we want God to do. We build our own empires and knock others down. We stare into the sky.

Luke reminds us in the opening chapter of Acts that Jesus had told them to wait in Jerusalem. Something big was going to happen and they wouldn't have to wait long. It would be of His making, not theirs. It would have kingdom significance, but not the kind they were thinking. The coming Spirit would be the birth of the Church and the awakening of worldwide mission. By the Holy Spirit, Jesus would soon be with them again.

Ponder
Matthew 16:21–28

Questions to Consider
In what ways have you waited for God to act in your life? What has made the waiting difficult? What made it easier to bear?

Closing Prayer
Forgive me, Lord, when I have turned from Your Great Commission to my own projects because it seems You have tarried too long. Please inspire me to take up the challenge again, and give me patience to wait for You to act at the right time. Amen.

DAY 27
Get on with it

Bible Reading
Acts 1:12–26

Daily Focus
Jesus' followers did what they could while they waited. With expectations repeatedly challenged and changed, they didn't know what to think or do anymore. Left with little option, they could only act on Jesus' final words to them: 'Do not leave Jerusalem, but wait for the gift my Father promised' (v4). They obeyed Jesus' instructions and stayed in Jerusalem, praying together. They waited. They prayed some more. Perhaps they thought or whispered to one another: *Somebody's got to do something!*

As they gathered together, the absence of one person is noticeable. Judas is described in graphic detail as having met his gory end in a field, where he took his life after betraying his master (v18). His own agenda ran so far ahead of God's plan that it destroyed his life. The believers decide to choose someone to replace Judas. They pray, discuss and draw up a shortlist. Then they cast lots, and Matthias takes the place of the twelfth disciple. They are ready. But still they wait. They've got on with what little they knew, and what little they could do. But they are limited. Waiting can be an active time. It can also be an anxious time.

For the Church in a waiting pattern for Jesus' return, we too can be uncertain sometimes about life, our faith in Jesus and what we are supposed to do while we wait. There are times when we cannot see what's ahead. There are times when the waiting seems to last forever. The temptation may be to disperse and to give up meeting together. The temptation may be to stop talking to Him because we've given up expecting to hear a response. In such times, we remember Jesus' promise that He is with us. If we don't hear from Him in a season, we do what we can. We get on with what we've been given to do. And we wait.

Advent is a time for remembering Jesus' past actions in our lives while we wait for His return. It's a time to remember what He last said to us, when we had clarity about life and mission. When we are stuck, either in our own lives or as a church community, a good thing to do is to gather (online in small groups if not physically) and pray. To wait. And then remember. What did Jesus last give you to do? What did He say? Remain true to that, get on with what you can, and you will be waiting with expectation. Waiting with expectation is the definition of hope. He will turn up, in His time.

Ponder
Luke 22:7–13

Questions to Consider
What are the Church's biggest distractions from carrying out Jesus' commission today? What are your biggest distractions? If you went back to the last clear word you heard from the Lord, what would you do differently? How can you wait for Jesus with expectation?

Closing Prayer
Lord, remind me of what it is You have given me to do. There are many ways I get distracted; help me to stay focused on Your mission while I wait for You. When I am confused, give me clarity; when I am wandering, bring me back home. Renew my hope in You. Amen.

DAY 28

Wind and fire

Bible Reading

Acts 2:1–13

Daily Focus

When we are able to gather to worship, we may not feel very powerful. We may feel out of step with the rhythms of the world as we sing a different song, and march to the beat of a different drum. Our expectations are often low. But today's Bible reading reminds us of who we are in God's plan.

As the disciples gathered together for Pentecost, something unimaginable happened. They grieved for Jesus, and they longed to have Him with them again. Unexpectedly, the presence of God – the Spirit of Christ Himself – came upon them with such power that it is described as tongues of fire. His return to them in the power and presence of the Spirit was unlike anything they could have anticipated. Jesus wasn't only *with* them; He was *in* them, working through them, binding them together and communing with their spirits. Jesus had been with them for a while but this comforter, this advocate, would be with them always. They would never have to say goodbye again. They would never be alone. The Lord will be their God and they will be His people.

Earlier in our Advent study, we saw how God scattered the people from Babel, varying their language. Now, by the Spirit, He empowers the believers with many tongues, so that the gospel can be shared to every tribe and language. Jerusalem was an incredibly diverse city that attracted people from across the known world. Suddenly, these visitors began to hear about the power of God in their own language by those who had no special linguistic ability or training. What was once scattered is drawn near. The good news of God is for everyone. Jesus, the light to the nations, is now proclaimed to all.

Unexpectedly, we are reminded that the good news of Jesus is not only for one culture or place or time. The Spirit offers an invitation to everyone and draws them in. No culture or ethnic background is excluded. Rather than making everyone the same, the Spirit elevates diversity by showing how unity is fully expressed by reconciling difference among Jesus' followers.

The Early Church would now learn to become a diverse but unified movement, as the Spirit brought men and women, Jews and Gentiles, from all classes and backgrounds together as God's people. Regardless of language or appearance, they were *all* followers of Jesus.

This week, when you gather for worship (online or in a building), remember that you are part of a 2,000-year-old movement that stretches around the world. The Holy Spirit makes us one body, whether we gather in Grantham or Ghana, Cardiff or Cambodia, Birmingham or Bolivia. The same Spirit who gave power to the Church to speak the good news of Christ in every language at Pentecost is the same Spirit who empowers us and sends us out today to share the hope of Christ. We are not alone. Christ is with us in presence and power.

Ponder
Revelation 7:9–17

Questions to Consider
How well does your church reflect the diversity of the community in which it is located? How have you seen the Spirit at work in bridging differences between people? How have you experienced the presence of the Holy Spirit in your life recently?

Closing Prayer
Lord, as You came in power at Pentecost, so come into my life now. Fill me afresh and remind me that You are with me every moment of every day. I can do all things through You because You give me strength. Amen.

DAY 29

He is with us

Bible Reading

Acts 2:14–24

Daily Focus

The disciples were about to discover that their grief over the absence of Jesus beside them would be replaced with joy by the presence of Jesus within them, through them and around them. They would now be bound to the Father, to Jesus and to one another with a closeness and commitment they could not have imagined. The Spirit would give them power in proclamation (vv14–41); discernment in decision-making (Acts 16:6); comfort in community (Acts 2:42–47); hope for healing (Acts 3:1–10); and peace in persecution (Acts 7:55). They need these things because ultimately, their kingdom expectations of comfort and privilege had to disappear and be replaced by the much more demanding mission of the kingdom of God.

What it means for God to be with us by His Holy Spirit is not always what we expect either. We have perhaps come to think of the Holy Spirit as our cosmic Santa Claus, doling out blessings at our request or even at our command. We take authority over the Spirit as though we can somehow tell God what to do. However, throughout Scripture, one thing is clear: all authority belongs to God alone. He will be who He will be. He is in control. His will is done, consistent with His character of holy love. We cannot tell Him what to do. And He will often do things that we do not, and cannot, understand.

What does it mean, then, to say that God is with us in the person and presence of the Holy Spirit? Perhaps it means for us the same thing as it did for the disciples. It means we are sent on a mission that we did not expect or ask for, but we are not without help. It means that the purposes for our lives are redefined in Christ, and we're about *His* eternal work and not simply our temporal expectations or desires.

The Holy Spirit does some mighty spiritual work: He seals our redemption (Eph. 1:13) and advocates for us before the Father (1 John 2:1). These are good gifts. The Holy Spirit is real and present in our everyday and sometimes messy lives too. Hard times come, and when they do, it's the Holy Spirit who comforts and convicts, draws us into community, renews our peace and restores our hope.

The Holy Spirit enables us to sing in the dark of the prison and hold the hands of the dying. He shouts when we are not listening and whispers when we are afraid. He enables us to speak truth to lies and cry justice to exploitation. The things He cares about are now ours to care about too. He shows us how things really are. They are not what we expect.

The Holy Spirit leads us just as Jesus Christ led His disciples. We can refuse to understand that 'God with us' means rewriting our expectations of God and ourselves. Or we can surrender, and have our lives caught up in a purpose that is greater than anything we could ask or imagine. It doesn't mean that it will be easy or that it will come with flowers. But it comes with the promise of the presence of Christ Himself.

Ponder
John 14:15–31

Questions to Consider
How has the Holy Spirit transformed your life? Where is He sending you on mission?

Closing Prayer
Lord, may the Spirit so fill me that I will overflow with Your love and share Your presence with those around me. Here I am. Send me. Amen.

DAY 30

Life expectancy

Bible Reading
Revelation 21

Daily Focus

In the Gospels, we read how Jesus came to be with us as a human being; in Acts, we learn that He is with us by His Spirit; and in Revelation we read about our future with Him in heaven. Revelation is full of apocalyptic imagery and prophetic insight but it is not just about the future. It is also about God being with us when we experience trials of all kinds and when we suffer. There is truly nowhere we can flee from His presence.

The final chapters of Revelation give us a glimpse of a glorious future when suffering, death, exploitation, racism and environmental destruction are no more. The glory of the Lord will shine so brightly that no other lights are needed. God Himself is the Temple where we will worship.

Once again, the diversity of people and nations is acknowledged. The nations will gather and will walk by the light of God. The kings of earth will be there too, just like the wise ones who came to see Jesus at His birth. Their glory will be brought into the holy city, and their honour will be caught up in the glory of God. The nations will share eternity.

When we are able to gather together as Christians, we may not feel significant. But we are making a clear political statement about our citizenship. While nations and diversity are part of God's design, their authority is subject to God. Being part of the Church means claiming that Jesus is Lord and affirming that our first loyalty is to Christ. Our citizenship ultimately belongs in heaven. While the picture we have in Revelation 21 is not yet fulfilled, we live in light of its reality in the present day. We are those who are gathered from every nation. We are those whose authority is submitted to the authority of Christ. If we claim His lordship over our lives, we must live according to His lordship.

To live with an eternal perspective is to live a life of expectancy. The most powerful aspect of this chapter in Revelation is that it allows us to see beyond the veil of this world to how things look from God's view. We live in light of the future, not to escape our present realities, but that we might be renewed in our courage to walk well with Jesus and others.

The light of God's presence is so bright that it shines from a heavenly future into the darkness of our world. We are its beacons. We are its lights. Knowing how the story ends doesn't lower our expectations or let us off the hook, rather it empowers us as ambassadors of reconciliation, to live out the realities of our kingdom citizenship. Even when it's hard. Even when it hurts. God is not only with us. He sends us.

He is making all things new.

Ponder
Philippians 3:17–21

Questions to Consider
What areas of life demand loyalty? How does the reality of God's future for His people impact how you live your life today?

Closing Prayer
Lord, remind me of my true citizenship with You. Help me not to seek security in the things of this world, but in Your everlasting kingdom. You are making all things new. In challenging times, help me to live in light of Your eternal presence. Thank You that You are always with me. Amen.

DAY 31

Come, thou unexpected Jesus

Bible Reading
Revelation 22

Daily Focus
We began this Advent study with the tree of life in the Garden of Eden, and we end with the tree of life in the heavenly city. In the Garden, there was a tree of life and a tree of the knowledge of good and evil. Now, there is only the tree of life. 'And the leaves of the tree are for the healing of the nations' (v2).

The river of life flows 'from the throne of God and of the Lamb' (v1), which reminds us of the Samaritan woman and the promise of living water Jesus made to her. Anyone may take this water and drink of it. It is the living water that wells up to eternal life. In this place, God's people once again walk with Him, they see His face, and they will be together for eternity.

The sense of healing after hurt is palpable here. Those who have sacrificed, those who have suffered, will see evil no more. There is hope, and there is promise. That Jesus will return and bring healing to the nations is not a false hope. It does not rest on our expectation. It rests on Jesus' own promise in two ways.

Firstly, it is an unexpected invitation to future hope offered to *all* nations and individuals. The healing of the nations is what the tree of life offers, renewing the life of faithful souls who have suffered persecution and tasted death. The invitation to come and drink of the water of life is for everyone who is thirsty. It is an open invitation that begins with Jesus and is passed on. It is a repeated invitation, though it is clear not everyone will respond. Those who *do* respond will receive life.

Secondly, future hope doesn't depend on our striving or wishful thinking, it depends on Jesus' promise. Several times He declares, 'I am coming soon' (vv7,12,20). If Revelation was written for tough times, the promise of Jesus is to hold on – the tough times won't last forever. *I am coming soon. Just a while longer. Wait with expectation. Wait with hope.*

Revelation 22 unfolds like a call and response between Jesus' declaration that He is returning soon and the agreement of all that this should be so. There is a responsive relationship between Jesus' promise and our expectation. Our expectation of Jesus' return is not based on our own internal inclinations, as if we could entice Him to return if only we plead hard enough. Our expectation of Jesus' return is birthed, renewed and encouraged by Jesus' statement that He *is* coming. That doesn't mean we are to focus solely on the end times, but that we are to live renewed in hope. He may not come as or when we expect. Believers are simply invited to lives marked out by expectation of Jesus' promise – the promise of His presence.

He will be with us. Just as He was at the beginning.

He who was with us at the beginning is with us still. And so shall He ever be.

Even so, come, thou unexpected Jesus.

Ponder
Luke 12:35–40

Questions to Consider
What difference does it make to your life that Jesus has promised to return? How have you been able to represent hope to others facing difficult times? What does hope look like for the world today?

Closing Prayer
Lord, give me the living water. Let me drink of it thirstily and deeply. Stay with me. Walk with me into a new year in hope and in the promise of Your eternal presence. Come, unexpected Jesus. Amen.

Group Study Notes

On the following pages, you will find group study suggestions for each of the four sessions contained in this study guide. The overall aim of these studies is to draw your group members into unexpected encounters with Jesus, and to respond to Him through discipleship and mission.

The notes and questions for each group study are focused on the same passages that have been explored in the daily Bible readings. The questions for discussion and further readings aim to build on what has been studied and draw out the themes further.

Each group study includes a summary of the Daily Focus notes from each session, a Bible reading that is related to the theme, six discussion starters and a thought to end the session.

Use the material in whatever way best suits the tone and needs of your group, whether you are meeting in person or online. Draw out some of the questions to explore the themes more deeply; spend some time in quiet reflection or a time of worship and pray for one another as you consider the relevance of the biblical material for the challenges and opportunities of life today. Feel free to adapt it in ways that will help your group members to deepen their understanding of God's presence and raise their expectations of the ways that God is with us this Advent season.

In whatever way you use this resource, I pray that you will be comforted, blessed, stretched and overwhelmed with the love of God and His deep desire to be with His people. Even when it's hard, even when it hurts, He meets us with unexpected hope.

SESSION ONE: GREAT EXPECTATIONS

Summary: In this first session, we considered whether we should expect anything from God, given the state of our world and our lives. We are perhaps surprised to discover that our default position with God is not a broken relationship, but wholeness. No matter how often God's people fail to live their lives in conformity to His will, He chases after them. Even when the world struggles under the enormous weight of the consequences of disobedience, He is never far away. In fact, He pursues us with relentless love.

Read
John 1:1–18

Discuss
1. What sorts of things have you expected from God in your life? What are your expectations of God this Advent?
2. What difference does it make to you that the first image for humanity in the Bible is life, not death?
3. In what ways has the earth suffered from the broken relationship between humans and God?
4. Do you have evidence of God showing up unexpectedly in difficult times? Are there times you expected Him and He didn't show up?
5. How have you responded to questions about God's love and presence this past year? How do the Bible readings in your study reassure you of His presence even when you haven't seen Him at work?
6. What does light look like in darkness today? What things can you or your church do together to speak hope to the world this Advent?

Ask someone to read John 1:1–18 again. As they read, invite the members of your group to imagine the light of Christ beginning to shine in their lives and in the world. They may wish to hold their hands open or spread their arms wide as an expression of their willingness to receive the presence of the unexpected Jesus.

SESSION TWO:
UNEXPECTED ARRIVAL

Summary: When Jesus arrives on the scene, He comes amidst diverse expectations but He challenges them all. He is not at all what many expect the Messiah to be.

This Advent, we are also challenged to receive this unexpected child who will change everything. God is truly with us.

Read
Isaiah 9:1–7

Discuss
1. Which study in this session resonated with you the most? Which character from session two can you relate to the best? Why?
2. In what ways did Jesus' arrival challenge the expectations people had of a messiah?
3. How does Jesus' arrival change your expectations of God?
4. What does it mean that Jesus is 'God with us' today?
5. Why do you think God chose to reveal Himself first to those on the margins of society?
6. Contrast the response of the wise men to the news of a king being born with that of Herod. How do you see these different reactions to Jesus played out among powerful people today?

As someone reads the Isaiah passage again, pause between each verse or section. Encourage your group members to prayerfully receive the comfort that the words bring. Invite them to focus on one phrase or title about Jesus that they find unexpected and encourage them to claim it as their own promise this Advent.

SESSION THREE: UNEXPECTED ENCOUNTERS

Summary: In this session, Jesus encounters several different people of the Bible in ways that are unexpected. These encounters are far more than casual meetings; they transform people and challenge the cultural wisdom of who is included and who is excluded in the plans of God.

Read
Acts 9:1–22

Discuss
1. Which unexpected encounter with Jesus resonated most with you? Why?
2. Why do you think Jesus always seems to challenge the status quo? How does He challenge yours?
3. How has Jesus showed up unexpectedly in your life? How did it change you?
4. Who is on your mind and heart that might benefit from an encounter with Jesus (maybe it's yourself)? Are you willing to pray that He would show up unexpectedly? What could that look like?
5. Do you sometimes have low expectations of Jesus? How does the Bible challenge your views?
6. How has Jesus unexpectantly turned up in the great difficulties of life this past year?

Invite your group members to pray silently for a few minutes, asking God to show them someone who needs an encounter with Jesus this Christmas season. Then invite them to pray that Jesus would meet with that person and draw them into His presence in a new and powerful way. It may be that the members of your group wish to pray for one another to encounter Jesus afresh this Christmas – beyond all their expectations.

SESSION FOUR:
UNEXPECTED RETURN

Summary: Advent is a time to consider not only the arrival on earth of God in Christ, but also a time to explore Jesus' promised return. In the person of the Holy Spirit, the presence of God comes again to His people. In the promise of Jesus' return to earth, and the culmination of all things, we anticipate, in the present, the hope of a glorious future. God's first and last words are not death, but life. God has always been with us. He will always be with us. Come, thou unexpected Jesus!

Read
1 Peter 3:1–18

Discuss
1. In what ways was the arrival of the Holy Spirit unexpected?
2. How did the arrival of the Holy Spirit challenge and change the disciples' expectations?
3. How do you respond when Jesus asks you to do something for the kingdom that might entail suffering rather than glory?
4. How would you describe hope for yourself and the world today?
5. In what ways can you bring the presence of God into the lives of people today who need light and life?
6. Why do we find a message of life and hope so unexpected in the world today? How can we live as people of hope and share it with authenticity today?

Spend some time praying for one another. Use the Bible reading for this session to guide your prayers. Ask God to reveal ways that you can demonstrate the reality of His unexpected presence to others. Before you close, spend a few moments encouraging each other with words of hope. Invite Jesus to turn up unexpectedly in your lives, renewing your hope for the future.

Notes...

There is more.
Take hold of it this Lent...

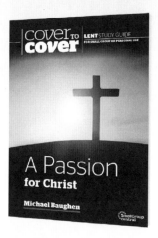

Find God in your
Every Day...

There's something for everyone!

Ten minutes with God every day can change your life.

Spend time seeking God's voice every day and see how your own faith deepens and grows, or encourage a friend or family member with a one-year gift subscription.

cwr.org.uk/brn

Courses and events

Waverley Abbey College

Publishing and media

Conference facilities

Transforming lives

CWR's vision is to enable people to experience personal transformation through applying God's Word to their lives and relationships.

Our Bible-based training and resources help people around the world to:
• Grow in their walk with God
• Understand and apply Scripture to their lives
• Resource themselves and their church
• Develop pastoral care and counselling skills
• Train for leadership
• Strengthen relationships, marriage and family life and much more.

CWR Applying God's Word
to everyday life and relationships

CWR, Waverley Abbey House,
Waverley Lane, Farnham,
Surrey GU9 8EP, UK

Telephone: **+44 (0)1252 784700**
Email: **info@cwr.org.uk**
Website: **cwr.org.uk**

Registered Charity No. 294387
Company Registration No. 1990308

Our insightful writers provide daily Bible reading notes and other resources for all ages, and our experienced course designers and presenters have gained an international reputation for excellence and effectiveness.

CWR's Training and Conference Centre in Surrey, England, provides excellent facilities in an idyllic setting – ideal for both learning and spiritual refreshment.